cloverleaf books™

Money Basics

Gabriel Gets a Great Deal

Lisa Bullard

illustrated by **Mike Moran**

M MILLBROOK PRESS · MINNEAPOLIS

For Sam —L.B.

Millbrook Press
A division of Lerner Publishing Group, Inc.
241 First Avenue North
Minneapolis, MN 55401 U.S.A.

Website address: www.lernerbooks.com

Main body text set in Slappy Inline 18/28.
Typeface provided by T26.

Library of Congress Cataloging-in-Publication Data

Bullard, Lisa.
    Gabriel gets a great deal / by Lisa Bullard ; illustrated by
Mike Moran.
        p.   cm. — (Cloverleaf Books™ : money basics)
    Includes index.
    ISBN 978-1-4677-0766-4 (lib. bdg. : alk. paper)
    ISBN 978-1-4677-1696-3 (eBook)
    1. Consumer behavior—Juvenile literature. 2. Consumer
education—Juvenile literature. I. Moran, Michael, 1957–
illustrator II. Title.
HF5415.32.B86 2014
640.73—dc23   2012039678

Manufactured in the United States of America
1 – BP – 7/15/13

TABLE OF CONTENTS

Chapter One

As Fast as a Cheetah

"The next school race is coming up on Friday. I really want to win! Can I get some Fast Kids shoes?" I asked Mom, pointing at the ad on TV. Mom shook her head. "Your old shoes are fine, Gabriel."

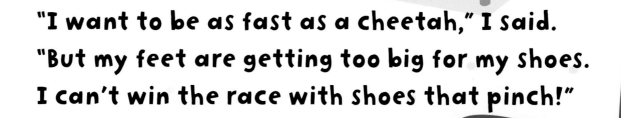

"I want to be as fast as a cheetah," I said.
"But my feet are getting too big for my shoes.
I can't win the race with shoes that pinch!"

Mom laughed. "OK, Cheetah. Let's look online to see what they cost."

"Here's the Fast Kids website," I said. "Can I order the shoes now?"

"Hold on," said Mom. "See how much they are? We can't spend more than $30.00! Try another website."

Does your family shop online?

"Here are some for $30.00!" I said.

Mom pointed to the screen. "See where it says '$10.00 for fast shipping'? You need the shoes soon. Shipping adds to the price. Keep looking for a better deal."

We checked more websites.
But Fast Kids always cost too much.

9

Chapter Two
Shopping Time

"Let's visit Mr. Smith's Shoe Store," said Mom. "We bought your old shoes there."

We drove to Mr. Smith's. They had Fast Kids in every color!

"Try them on. And take a careful look to make sure they're as good as you think," said Mom.

Mom liked them as much as I did. But she didn't like the **$38.00** price tag.

"They'll be on sale next month," said Mr. Smith. "Can you wait?"

I shook my head.

The shop next door sold newspapers. Mom bought one and gave it to me. "Look for ads. That's another way to find a great deal," she said.

The Shop More Store had the biggest ad. It said, "Sale! Sale! Sale!"

"Here's one," I said. "Shop More's ad has a coupon. It says, '$10.00 off all shoes through this weekend.' Can we go?"

Fast Kids shoes usually cost $38.00 at Shop More. How much will they cost with the coupon?

Chapter Three

A Hard Choice

Shop More had bikes, backpacks, and bananas.
But they didn't have Fast Kids shoes.

"Sold out," said a sign.

"I'll never be cheetah fast," I said.

"How about these other shoes?" Mom pointed. "They aren't as flashy as Fast Kids. But they'll last until your feet get even bigger. And they cost only **$20.00** with the coupon. We'd have enough money left to go to Pizza King."

$30.00

Where's your favorite place to shop?

I just couldn't choose. I love the games at Pizza
King. Did that mean I should buy these shoes? But
what if they made me as slow as a sloth? Should
I wait for the Fast Kids sale at Mr. Smith's? We'd
have another school race in a month.

"If you're not sure, it's better to go home and think longer," said Mom. "But decide before your toes pop out of your old shoes!"

If you were Gabriel, what would you choose?

Chapter Four
The Best Deal

On the way home, I had an idea. "Can we check the thrift store?" I asked. "I got a football there for only **$2.00**."

"Good idea," said Mom. "But remember, you never know what they'll have."

Guess what I found at the thrift store? Not Fast Kids, but something just as good: Cheetah Speed shoes! The same kind that Manuela wore to win last month's race.

"They're only $10.00 because they've already been worn," said Mom. "But they're still in good shape. How do they fit?"

"Not one pinch!" I said. "Finally, I found a great deal!"

But do you want to know the best deal of all? I won the race!

Make Your Own Ad

Ads try to talk people into buying or doing a certain thing. Gabriel saw Fast Kids shoes in a TV ad. The ad asked him to buy the shoes. He found a coupon in a newspaper ad. The ad and the coupon were meant to talk him into buying shoes at a certain store. Now you can make your own ad to give to your family or friends! All you need is paper and markers or crayons.

First, think up something that you think other people would like to buy. It could be a toy, a kind of cereal, some cool shoes, or anything else you can imagine.

Next, draw a picture of your item on a sheet of paper. Try to make it look as good as you can so that others would want to buy it. For example, you might show a computer game with lots of friends gathered around together playing it.

Next, come up with something to say about your item. It should be something that would make people want to buy it. This could be something like, "Best toy of the year!" for a toy. Or "Yummy and good for you!" for a cereal. Think about ads you see on TV or the writing you see on toy boxes to help you think of what to say.

Finally, add a coupon to your ad if you want to. The coupon could offer a dollar off or free shipping.

When you have finished making your ad, give it to your friends or family members. Ask them if your ad would make them want to buy your item.

GLOSSARY

ad: short for advertisement. An ad is something that is used to try to get people to buy or do a certain thing.

choose: to pick between different things

coupon: a slip of paper that you can cut out from a newspaper ad or print out from online to get a special deal. Some cell phones also allow you to get coupons on the screen. You can show them when you buy something to get a special deal.

online: on the Internet, or being connected to a network of computers

shipping: mailing something

thrift store: a place where used items are resold

website: pages on the Internet that go together and are put online by one person or group

ANSWER KEY

page 9: $40.00

page 13: $28.00

BOOKS

Cleary, Brian P. *A Dollar, a Penny, How Much and How Many?* Minneapolis: Millbrook Press, 2012.
Rhyming text and goofy illustrations introduce U.S. bills and coins.

Larson, Jennifer S. *Do I Need It? Or Do I Want It? Making Budget Choices.* Minneapolis: Lerner Publications Company, 2010.
This book teaches you more about making smart spending choices.

Salzmann, Mary Elizabeth. *Money for Toys.* Edina, MN: Magic Wagon, 2011.
Follow along as Olivia makes choices about saving and spending money for toys.

WEBSITES

Safety Land
http://www.att.com/Common/images/safety/game.html
This website from AT&T teaches you how to stay safe while you are shopping online.

Spending Smarts: Ten Super Shopping Tips
http://pbskids.org/itsmylife/money/spendingsmarts/article8.html
This website from PBS Kids gives you lots more information about how to be a smart shopper.

Wise Pockets World
http://www.umsl.edu/~wpockets
This website has stories to help you learn about earning money and buying things.

LERNER SOURCE
Expand learning beyond the printed book. Download free, complementary educational resources for this book from our website, www.lerneresource.com.